NARCISSUS

Bagoo

ISBN: 978-1-915079-38-1

Cover designed by Aaron Kent

Edited and typeset by Aaron Kent

Broken Sleep Books Ltd
Rhydwen,
Talgarreg,
SA44 4HB
Wales

Contents

Narcissus

Andre Bagoo

I am another now and yet the same.
— James Joyce, *Ulysses*

Epistemology of the Closet

You make art of me,
turn hate into the first poem
of a book you author
deep inside a closet
of sleep.

Count sheep
dreamer,
I authored you.

I looked and saw
a flower that looked and saw
itself
a flower that saw
itself—

nightmare, petals

stone

Firsts

The poem starts
after the fight
when I go
down on my knees
and caress
the flower
of your forgiving
cock
remembering
the first time
we kissed
empty streets
confronting us
with our selves.
When I'm laid
in bed I see
you most clearly
but I see him too
all the versions of you
jumbled up like the
Pitch Lake's detritus—
cans, branches, minerals.
I didn't realise
there would be
so many firsts.

   First kiss:
her lips absolutions
for sins not yet
enjoyed,
for being
unreachable.

        Then,
the beach that yawned
with serene rage
and spit   a man at me
his hole
harboured
my fealty
held me
until I saw
in him a mirror
a wet face.

        Then,
the professor whose
library was a manifesto
of yearning
for whetted fingers,
for marble hardness
and I made room for
his

a new country
where every day
was the first day
of something
and every night
seagulls flew tall
as dreams
over fields singed
by birds-of-paradise
all of the new
all of the old
knowledge a
budding candle,
candle turning
to blaze.

I didn't realise
there would be
so many:
days clear as
coming out
days of
coming out
and coming out
and coming out
because we are
all of us
stars that come out
too soon for twilight
too late for dawn
and even after
they die
there might
still be
light.

Chapter Two

That morning the radio was playing a song that felt familiar even if I didn't know the words, didn't understand the language. I recognized the grainy static, the tinny voice, the muffled beats as though they were my thrumming heart, as though they were the rain that had fallen last night on the galvanize roof as you slept on top of me smelling of too much cologne, your two Venezuelan friends huddled on a bed in the corner, and something rising in their chests like bread dough, breaths soft clouds now floating into the air as I dream out of the house, the yard, I pass the chickens, I pass the dogs and someone follows me—am I remembering correctly?—I have a strange feeling, as I did the night before, a feeling that there are sagas inside me waiting to be written, epics as heavy as the gold chain you wore as you thrust into me and I tried to muffle my moans because it was all so sketchy and even as I surrendered to pleasure I still thought the weight of your pendant slapping my flesh was like the weight of something I might one day carry, some foundation stone, some temple. I didn't know where the taxi stand was and I asked a man who gave me directions then decided he would walk the short distance with me. Later, I roamed Port of Spain knowing everybody could tell what I'd done, could smell the smoke from the club on me, could look into my eyes and see the drag queen, the pole dancer, the small room with walls of mirrors, the gravelled yard outside on which footsteps crunch like whispered secrets and groups of friends look at each other cautiously, from a distance, because tomorrow is the question.

Elegy

They dumped her in Mandela Park
They stabbed him in his elegant living room
They lured him on Grindr, sent him flying off
They raped him with a juicy cane stalk
They beat him in the green Savannah
They said no motive was determined
They said no motive was determined
They said no motive was determined
They said no motive was determined   a cliff
They consulted with the churches
They mobilised against queer agendas
They marched to protect the family
They legislated their bigotry
They voted for the homophobic party
They said there was no evidence of hate crimes
They mouthed the national watchwords: *Discipline, Production, Tolerance*

Chapter One

                                        He
                made up his mind to leave

                                he could

                                        disappear

                                in

        the wind
                        Cane had been the destiny of his father,
                                                        indentured
                in the burning sun.

he thought:
                        London, perhaps,

        Canada
                        He   was

                        a carpet of soft petals.

Heaven, Charing Cross

It is Almighty God I see in this echoing club
        Echo.   *Club.*
that sits next to a river of London gin and tonic.
        Echo.   *Tonic.*
Behold, my true mirror: these people dancing
        Echo.   *Sing.*
as though parts of a collective wet dream.
        Echo.   *Dream.*
What flows between us in this room, in smoky levels?
        Echo.   *Levels.*
Nothing. Everything. The last time I saw Father
        Echo.   *Her.*
he held out a book like a Carnival Bookman,
        Echo.   *Man.*
who records all sins. What can the will enjoy?
        Echo.   *Joy.*
Here is the way to cross the water, to become
        Echo.   *Come.*
bright, blossoming lasers. We will be flight.
        Echo.   *Light.*

Echo

is   this

              river

        my true mirror

               my

                       last

          book

Gilgamesh Love Cento

— from Herbert Mason's 1970 translation

Gilgamesh was king
Enkidu was an animal

Calling his name, calling him from sleep
Or from some pleasureful moment
On a foreign street

                  into a land
That promises a vision or the secret
Of one's life,
      free of voices,   voice
Calls out like a voice from childhood,
Reminding him he once tossed in dreams

                  Pleasure
Seemed to grow from fear for Gilgamesh.
As when one comes upon a path in woods
Unvisited by men, one is drawn near
The lost and undiscovered in himself

Some called the forest "Hell", and others "Pleasure"

And they had no time to call it names,
Except perhaps "The Dark"
            a place at the edge of the forest
    shelter for their sleep

His single stroke could cut a cedar down

The way the sea contorts under a violent squall
I'll serve you as I served the gods
I'll build you houses from their sacred trees

On John William Waterhouse's Echo and Narcissus, *1903*

Firstly, quite clearly Narcissus is a bottom, what with the practiced arch of that lower back, bum in the air, the way he crumples his shawl like you'd crumple a bedsheet while getting railed. Secondly, Echo is so over being a beard. Thirdly, can we talk about how creepy the reflective water is? They say every mirror is false because it shows us our reversed face. A photograph shows us what we really are. Unseen in the painting are the bulbs of flowers that retract beneath the soil in winter, each a penis ensilked in foreskin.

Narcissus

BULBS

burrow deep each year into making it harder to breathe once more. harder
to rise through the angelic orders. of dirt and rock for whom there is no
springtime. only the suffocation of i dig my fist into this earth. just this.
alone. buried here in darkness. could be the whole thing. layers wrapped
in night-like obstacles to understanding. how could it be that i am from this
ground yet you are also from this ground? how could they know what is
encased in us? every mind hides itself

STEMS

will the soil remember? will the soil remember them? desires roused by
lute or horn. seeking to grasp or grasping. servants of the bow-and-arrow
god. alike and kin. alike and false. naked. succulent. hollow. the pointed
tips of fingers carrying nostalgia for things they cannot seed. let there be
madness in their ambition: their sword-like being. let the people panic
at the sight of this green army of lances. echoes of government. (here she
withdraws into wild places. among foliage. in caves. and on mountainsides.
bone to stone. flesh to voice)

FLOWERS

some species are extinct. small mouths opening. nature re-entering itself. hoping
to renew. a center. white miasma of stormy days. of mobile phone screens. of
pages for poems. sudden ripples. faces turning away like wind vanes. deciding.
do you know echo's flesh was ripped apart by shepherds? once, i lay in a field
with a man beside me, his beard a furred country. with him i travelled to the
mouth of a river in a dream of a river and found all that is left of the body is a
flower

Song of Night Flowers
— for Colin Robinson

Into Paradise came the twinks,
slender deer with big eyes and big dicks
some hungry for the daddy at the bar
but too proud to seem wanting.
Then came those who didn't know
how the night would end, who
didn't know who would drive them home,
who didn't foresee the fast car, the black leather,
his hand on the gearstick, wind blowing through hair like revolution—
Then the bears and the cubs who knew
how to handle their liquor. Then the UWI students
for whom this was a tutorial on love.
Then came those who didn't know why they had come,
who stood in a dark corner and watched and maybe
that was enough. Then there were those who knew
exactly what they came for: Marilyn Monroe
standing in the good light; the Muscle Marys with
boastful biceps who smelt fresh as tuberoses;
the political aspirants oozing the charm of the
unreachable; the lesbian couple who came cause
their friend Duayne had a rough week and he
wanted to get crunk; the twunks and the otters
who were working on their bodies and counting
calories but today was a cheat day; the closet
dancers outing themselves after a few drinks,
pretending to be oblivious as the gayelle circled
around them; the couples holding hands;
the quietly respectful fuck buddies. They
did not know what had been here before—
what stood on this site, the laughter and tears.
They did not know what they could not know—
in a matter of months, the club would close,
the owner would leave, would marry a man in
Canada, the tables would stop turning,

the soca would stop playing. Who could say
whether some seed had already been planted
in soil ploughed by dancing feet, and we
might all wake up one day like lovers the morning after
and know: it had been, it could be again—

Flying Termites

what is wood
 but water?
swirling as
we swarm
   solid veins
   hidden
chambers
full, brooding
  galleries
   behind bark
  what is a door
 but a way?
the door
  in our way
  in our way
we devour it
  mouth meeting
   mouth a river
  tracing hunger
   knots, throats
what are bodies
   but wings?
  swinging doors
crowning kings
  nuptial flight
we multiply
   by night
 the nest no
longer good
 enough wood
never bright
 enough no
door better
   than light

Mora Trees
— a found poem from JS Beard

Viewed from the air, the canopy of Mora forest has the same undulating but continuous character of the waves of the sea.

The bark of the Mora tree is brownish and scaly, about 5—7 mm. thick, hard and tough.

The blaze is pale brown, the sapwood white, the heartwood deep red-brown.

The timber is hard, and though resistant to termites it is susceptible to fungus attack and therefore not durable when in contact with the ground.

Mora is evergreen. Flush leaves are pinkish brown in colour. Flushing takes place over the whole tree at once and usually over the whole forest also, at which times the canopy is a striking sight.

Shrub, field and ground layers in the forest are composed almost exclusively of young Mora seedlings and saplings, which form a dense, scarcely penetrable growth.

Mora forest as a whole seeds abundantly every year, though individual seeds may not do so.

The seed, which falls during the second part of the wet season (November— December) is a heavy bean about 7—10 cm. in length and weighing nearly 0.5 kg.

It naturally falls only beneath the parent tree, but the seedling produced is vigorous and able to stand heavy shade, so that the forest floor is densely carpeted with Mora seedlings.

Mora seems to have reached Trinidad just as earth movements made it an island. Mora then became cut off from its original home in Guiana, but as forest conditions were returning in Trinidad it was able to establish itself there successfully.

During Pleistocene times the area that is now Trinidad was a part of continental South America and consisted for the most part of a vast, level plain, which was co-extensive with the great llanos of the Orinoco.

The aboriginal Indians in British Guiana are known to use Mora seeds as a food. It seems quite reasonable that wandering hunting parties of these aborigines may have carried supplies of Mora seeds on occasion about the Trinidad forests and have abandoned them at campsites, where they germinated and initiated a new block of Mora forest.

It is just possible that Indians may have carried the seeds to Paria beach. Otherwise no rational explanation seems possible. This point is the northernmost in the distribution of Mora.

It must be a matter of difficulty for any seedling other than a Mora to come up through the dense mass of Mora saplings. The species thus establishes initially a thick ground carpet of its own seedlings which maintain an almost exclusive right to succession in the forest. Once such a carpet has been laid down it is only a question of waiting for the older trees to die before a gregarious Mora forest comes into being.

Ti Marie

UNTOUCHED

In this savannah,
        trees have walked
  away, leaving an expanse
          of green loneliness in which
 you crawl and creep, each of
        your limbs like one of the boys
 who almost loved me: bashful,
        sensitive, afraid, leaves opening
only by the night, thorny, purple-
        flowered, strong stemmed:
  Ti Marie, Misé Marie, morivivi,
        touch-me-not, shame plant,
  Mary Shut Your Door. Each
        leaf, each name, the same
  lover, spread in poor soil,
        where once cane was
  grown and slaves knew.

TOUCHED

Breathing like this
should be good enough.
We are not separate. We
die hundreds of times each
day. We are born hundreds of
times each day. Each breath
opens us, our leaves spread
out to kiss the darkness. Then,
like lungs, we close to the
touch. We are born. We lay down.
Our legs spread wide by hands
of men who don't love us.
Our legs are trussed after they have
touched us. Coffle logic.
Leaf orientation. I want to kiss
the married man but he will
not let me. In Trinidad,
do not trust plants.

A CURE

for rashes for insomnia walks
with own sky the leaves for

indigestion for tabanca the
stems the creeping can

change walks the soil but
cannot cure men here his

mother didn't approve of this
lifestyle is a wallpaper a

tablecloth for snake bites rapid
plant movements sleep leaf he

didn't approve of this lifestyle
orientation sleep foliage closes

he really loves me during darkness
and reopens in light sleep unique

response to touch he couldn't
imagine this life is something

you start ideal for experiments
regarding plant memory bashful

shrieking invasive and someone
else finishes species petioles are

also prickly he wasn't that way see
cotyledons filaments pink to

lavender he wasn't interested he
was saying yes to everything except

this he had a boyfriend he was a
perfect boyfriend he touching warming

blowing shaking was too good for
me his grandmother didn't approve

he didn't know himself compound
leaves fold inward and droop I am

for ague for anomie for opening and
closing doors Venus Fly Trap

the plant that elaborates the
boys who almost loved me

Night Nurse

I.

First one stitch then two
rising through keloid flesh like dreams.
My body knows before I do.

My scar yields things to you,
a fine blue thread, left behind by the nurse
who smiles, who sees
how well my wound heals.
He says, "Soon you will be free."

Time is flesh: all we were, all we are,
all we will be. The body, it knows.
The future writes our dreams.

II.

time passes and
all I have is the poem

III.

Floors yellow, walls yellow, doctors
in photographs with successful teeth,
mudslides on the news, the television
in the corner is the constant witness,
words here bend into medical tests.
What disease? How many kidneys?
Meteors crash onto green chairs
families crater then settle into
waiting (time) waiting (service)
weighing the options: live or die?
A soul or no soul? Maybe the soul
is like the line of a poem depending
on what's before, what's coming,
then going somewhere else. Stories.
Exit is the clearest sign. The magazine
rack has not been touched in years.
A scrawl on the wall asks of its origin,
perhaps a child left it behind. A child
who was waiting to find out if
Mother died, his cousins shivering
under blankets. The room before love.

Mealy Bug Sonnet

all they get, they get by chance
and multiply in ignorance
wedded white, they grow between bliss
they grow, this peacetime upheaval, grow
outbreak of dandruff in cotton tranches
behold: diamond dew (a mistaken view)
'til the whole plant is ensnowed
fossil leaves curled like Mother's hem
Texas sage made fungus, at last transformed
from a thing living to a thing possessed
this is how it blooms, like mushrooms in
the Savannah after Christmas rain
this is how it moors, to wide open fields,
unexplored hills in the distance, grief

Carnival Mask

Upon your face I find my meaning
Against the elements, your body my standard, I am
Cut for you to breathe, my eyes fearful symmetries, my
Paper skin long hardened, forever bent to your
Imperfect form; the jaws of life, the spires of
My horns are effortless and proud.

Heavy is the crown, heavier when
Discarded—dumped in dust, lost among the
Used-up cinders, my beaten shape of ash.
Yet, next year you will see. You cannot leave
Me. Like a man scorned, I bide my time.
For the mask is really all of your fear—
The mask is what you do not wear.

Carnival Bat

my roll cage my inside out gold-leaf wings gasoline licked
/crumpled flight flight purpled and faild e I flucked
transparent paths rag hanging limp imp on stage

dancing on stage in front of everybody still
no body, black and transparent
whipped, metronomed, corbeauxed,
dropped between night and day
a fruit soca, soul turned upside
this down hanging rag oil laugh

The Water in the Pond Considers Narcissus

He looks at me and sees right through me, as if I am nothing, as if he could live without me. I bathed him each day, moistly kissing the rise of his flesh, slapping his limbs then falling away, down and down lower and cooler. The surface is all he sees. Not the way I labour to raise his own face back up to him, not my rippled laughter, my silver mechanics. Nothing.

Now I know what I must do.

When next he leaves, I will replace his face. I will lay still and let him come over me: the sun. The sun. I will rise. My vapours will take back everything. And all that will be left is the empty gash in the soil where I once made my bed, where I offered him all of my soul, my molecules, where I let him step into me, deep, his buried flesh rejoicing. Instead he will step and find nothing but a grave.

Narcissus

in this white bed all things are made
into a dream in which I fall into a lake
a small pond in which I disappear
 or am met, each day, with a new man
  one with a hare lip
   one with accusations
  eyes saying no no
  mumbling self-loathing
 mirror-mad I see them through a window
that makes itself into a loving opening
 to some place that is a conspiracy
  designed to keep me from myself
      who are they? who are they?
       which is to say,
   after the beating my world crumbled
I couldn't show anyone my face
more of them began to appear
 one with a trust problem
 another callous with friends
 the shadows of Plato's Cave
                         slid up the bedroom wall
          the past troubling the curtains, bodies
              buried among lace. They took
    my father's watch
which I would wear long after it stopped
 my father who knew,
        who saw, who told me yes

           long after
         he rose from the water
      having changed like the ship of Theseus
in rippled light,   he rose, pebbled tombstones
      left beneath the surface, each marking small drownings
        fallen masks   tiny surrenders
  to the randomness of water, to the crystalloid silk

of each new body joyfully swum into,
    and he looked back at me   naked
and I saw   anew
 and   in this wet circle
    I loved him   you

      and we knew

Mirrors

1943

The island is twenty-seven miles from the coast of
California, half the size of Tobago, with roaming bison
and goats, dense forest, unspoilt cliffs, bays of
yachts tranquil as lilies on the blue water. It was fitting
she ended up here, in a town called Avalon, where instead of
Excalibur, her destiny was forged. The house on the hill had
a view: here she discovered the Pacific. His name was Jimmy,
he had the softest hair she ever felt. They would watch
the sun, now Westward of her West, fall to the sea.
Where it led she would be. When she packed his lunch
for work, there would be a note inside: 'Dearest Daddy—
When you read this I'll be asleep and dreaming of you.
Love and kisses, Your Baby.' Later in the day, she would
walk Muggsy among the fruit-bearing trees, his black nose
sharp to the directions of life. The day Jimmy
left, she cried into the mirror on the wall.

1960

She cried into the mirror on the wall of her trailer
and remembered Jimmy and wondered if she'd
end up here had he not left her: in a desert, staring back
at something tarnished. But a mirror always lies.
She could not see what cameras saw:
what certainty there was in life was on her face,
a big screen that said what she was—what was she?
The Director called for her and on the set, mustangs
ran wild, each carrying war inside. One, a scaffold of bones,
fell behind the herd. The men threw lassos and caught it,
tied its bony ankles. Its frenzy gave way to a resigned peace
as unastonished hands turned it into dog food and she
remembered the flamingos, the macaws, the candy shop, the
house on the hill back when Marilyn Monroe was
Norma Jeane and she lived on the island named after
St Catherine, whom the world murdered.

Echo

Each day, the mirror told her lies,
but today's was a revelation: a man
peering through the window. Most
days it was a woman who appeared —
Cathy with her cupcakes, the cougar
with the face of melted wax, the lady
with the grey hair. But this man had
eyes that were habours. She invited
him over, but he would not come.
He would not come.
He would not come.
Until, she gave up on this stalker
who had a way of looking right through her.
They said he liked men.
But she didn't believe him beyond her.
Who was it who said: "Life —
I am of both your directions"?
She wondered if this unreachable man
was really herself, a book left open by
an absent schoolmaster.
When love was out of the question,
at last she saw her reflection.

Echo

Each day, the mirror told him lies,
but today's was a revelation: a lady
peering through the window. Most
days it was a man who appeared—
Carl with his plaid, the silver fox
with the face of melted wax, the professor
with the grey hair. But this woman had
eyes that were invitations. He made her
promises, but he could not go.
He could not go.
He could not go.
Until, he grew tired of pretending
that he could see and love her.
They talked about him, they all did.
Were the rumours all true?
Who was it who said: "Life—
I am of both your directions"?
He wondered if this unbreakable pane
was really his fate, a closet with locks
forever untested.
When love was out of the question,
at last he saw his reflection.

On James Bidgood's Pink Narcissus, *1971*

How's this for a nature poem: for eight years he filmed it in his cramped apartment. He made all the props. He made all the sets, including one public bathroom in which the urinals were made of foamcore. He devised all the special effects. He got neighbourhood hustlers to make up his cast who basically stood around showing off their bulges. There's no storyline to speak of: the only plot being followed is horniness. This is an Oulipo poem. This is something made beautiful by constraint. The only light in this world is purple and pink and blue and I almost forget to notice the weird brownface bit. I do notice the diaphanous veil and the belly dancer playing helicopter with his impressive member. There is one part where he recreates an entire city street and guys walk around wearing condoms on their semis and then someone with a really pert ass seems to be fondled by plastic foliage before getting soaked in the rain. All of this in his apartment, which was his mind.

On Salvador Dalí's Metamorphosis of Narcissus, *1937*

Looking, your metaphors crack open
Looking, your metaphors crack open
Until flowers bloom and stones are dogs
Until flowers bloom and stones are dogs
Your metaphors crack open, until
Flowers bloom and stones are dogs

Someone praying, a sprinter at a starting line, a hand, an egg
Someone praying, a sprinter at a starting line, a hand, an egg
How the fingers hold the testicle
How the fingers hold the miracle
A sprinter at a starting line, a hand, an egg, how
the fingers hold the testicle

The flowers are dying
The flowers are dying
Ash clouds
Ash clouds
Flowers are dying, ash
clouds

Until ash clouds bloom and stones are flowers
the praying will be forever dying – a miracle how metaphors crack
open at someone starting a lie, a sprinter, a hand, the testicle,
an egg the fingers hold,
your dogs,
looking

Echo

This was a landscape locked in amber
The cliffs and gullies of his chest
The floodplain of his lower torso
The promontories of his arms
I'd voyaged through it unseeing for so long
Like a man stepping through the sea
Not seeing the water's bright writing

Unwrit, underwritten: the fossils oozing
From his ground. Each night he came I saw
Nothing. Each night we gave chase to
That which gnawing mouths divined.
Down, low, worshipping evasions
Until he drilled and drilled to a core that
Was molten and what was found in me,
Was found in him, was himself.

Woodbrook Eclogue

concrete walls tall walls small walls
leaning walls

dreamy walls fussy walls grumpy walls
apolitical walls

walled walls open walls holy walls
slutty walls

at least we write poems
and birds
moons the shape of fish
Spanish herbs in pots
love them all
the strangers and the dead
up against falling

jasmine walls crumbled walls squatting walls
forever walls

Cherry

Like the time I ate lipstick and mom thought this child crazy. She was always like the sea. Angry, swallowing people who just wanted a little dip. Beware of water, she would warn me, citing my widow's peak. The barber asked me if I normally shaved it off. I said no. He said okay. Then he looked at me. Then he looked at me in the mirror looking at him looking at me in the mirror looking at him and said he was going to take it all away. I swore he was Frank Ocean and when he started to sing songs later on I fell unto the tiled floor. He swept mother right out of me. She said I would die of fire.

Because the Sky Is Lighter Than Paper,
a Manifesto of Feathers

I.

blue because my wings are the bookman's pages

blue because the island is holy, the wind high

blue as in azure as in cadmium as in noise

blue and black because kisses hurt

blue when they saw me, they saw us

blue the night we were walking home, josh, you and i, and the thugs

blue the night outside the art gallery when they chased us, unwing'd

II.

blue like mary's robes

blue like the altar boy gown i wanted because it was fabulous

blue when they threw me out the church, and i dreamt of jesus truly

blue and the cherub has turned

blue and the angel has turned

blue into blue into krishna

blue and i saw him one day in my dreams

blue shirt of blue school uniform

blue invisibility

blue, he touched my spine and flutes sang in me

blue, both mirror and mute

blue the walls, the stones, the tomb

blue once, but now *coolitude, créolité* blue

blue *indienocéanisme,*

blue *antillanité, négritude, batiment* not batty man

blue for the way my heroes are dying but

blue mad for the second coming

blue veins on every dick i ever sucked

blue power, blue notes, the currency of

blue, melodies, you, rubber orchestras, true

blue blood & blue-collar &

blue scrubs fighting red coats

blue ink for blue manifestos of

blue feathers, disobedient walls, graffiti is

blue, jab molassie is

blue, and maybe—

the second coming

The Death of Eric Williams, Whose Iron Grip Ruled a Country

It was suicide

It was murder

It was an accident

It was an accidental suicide

It was an accidental murder otherwise known as manslaughter

It was medical malpractice

It was a clerical error

It was supernatural intervention

It was the CIA

It was Moscow

It was the Black Power Movement

It never happened

It was none of the above

Pablo Escobar's Hippos

After the raid, they found them in the hacienda
Four big, bare ungulates, even-toed, porpoise-like
Worthy cousins to whales, each a quatrain of wallowing.
They slipped away, lost to cathedrals of night.

They re-emerged, some time later, dozens of them,
Volcanic islands being born,
Basalt flecks on the water at Magdalena,
Steamy and slick and legion.

A feral species culls what it finds.
A feral plant becomes a noxious crop.
Pablo Escobar, they say, has come back.
And the world is one long murder.

Ornella

She knew—a camera phone is a shield against the onslaught of lies and rumours, she saw what was happening, the savagery trained on their bodies, she thought of the child in her belly, how one day that could be him lying in the dirt next to the highway or slumped in a car with his birthday cake or shot in the back with his hands up in surrender. *Not worth it*, her mother said, *Come back inside*. But what kind of world was it when police could shoot an unarmed man then say he asked for it, then shoot the protestors, then silence their critics, when million-dollar CCTV networks see nothing, when body cameras don't work, when authorities have no authority, when they probe and investigate and inquire and inquest and still cannot see what phone cameras can: son after son after son, the same poem written again and again, lines

cut like lives sliced, the poet deranged, images of blood making halos around smashed heads that will never dream again, and after each death, each unjust killing, the Cheshire Cat Commissioner of Police, brings a red rose to the funeral and puts it on the casket. Ornella, her Italian name, meaning flowering ash tree, said to come from *aurum*, the Roman equivalent of gold.

Hurricane Erasures

The sky, it seems, would pour down stinking pitch
— Shakespeare, *The Tempest*
They'd blow the world away
— Virgil, *The Aeneid (tr. Robert Fangles)*

CATEGORY 3

my son

Our revels now are

melted into
fabric

the   globe itself
shall dissolve

Leave   We
are

weakn   troubled:
disturb'd   infirm

turn   walk,

CATEGORY 1

                                          father lies;
his

                                                 eyes:
                                     fade
                             sea-change

                                 ring his knell

CATEGORY 2

                 the isle is full of
                             hurt
             a thousand twangling instruments
hum   and sometime voices
             wake

     clouds   open and show riches
        drop   on me   wake
          dream

CATEGORY 5

a vast cave
howling
chains them down in their dungeon, shackled fast.
They bluster in protest, roaring round their prison bars
with a mountain above them all
hurling
Fearing

binding
Free

Down they crash

heaving   killer breakers
    rolling towards the beaches   crews   shouting,
    cables screeching—   cloudbanks blotting out
        the sky, the   day   the Trojans' sight
    as pitch-black night comes   down on the sea
        thunder crashing pole to pole, bolt on bolt

        blazing across heavens—death, everywhere

Tropopause — a Cento

such sheets of fire, such bursts of horrid thunder, and then, again,
such groans of roaring wind and rain I never
such a night
as this
a lowness but
a poor bare forked animal
a small deer
a traitor
a storm as his bare head
such children
such a fellow
such sacrifices
such addition as your Honours
such conditions
such unnatural degree
such a tongue
daughter
unconstant starts are we
such dispositions
such need to hide itself
such a monster
such a king

Secondary Circulation – a Cento

When the wind works against us in the dark,
And pelts

roadside flowers, too wet for the bee
Come over the hills and far with me
And be my love in the rain.

Cento for a Poet from the British Virgin Islands

                                    skyward

What are poems but prayers?   birds always find their way back
        home   but home is   nowhere—a memory; a never was
        Do wings remember   the air   my beard grows wild
    I forget   goodbye   comes in the languages
I cannot remember   coffee   grounds wet like earth   when I am gone
        don't tell anyone I am gone   the clouds no longer look
    like drowned bodies but I can no longer trust my mother's histories
        The sun sank like a hurled stone   you will find your way
Everywhere is song   the hollow wail of galvanise tearing away

    from the rafters   still, long after the storm had taken him
        They say he held the door   the thing that breaks you is
                        all there is

In Transit

He crossed the border seeking warmth. Instead,
everything was wet. A storm struck the

ship like damnation. He saw tide foam round
his ankles, stars hung water-sunk, while the

boat rocked to waves mouthing mantras: I am,
I am, *I was*. But at dawn, the world was

a dream of clear sea, the sun made rippling
signatures. At his desk, his pen was fluent

as rivers. His words, like sails, sought harbour.
When they reached Naples it was a new masque.

His final costume was hard to shed: real life in
quarantine, the Spanish Steps silent and steep,

as nearby, Roman fountains gurgled eclogues
and tourists completed their idle ablutions.

Torn Lace

for Shivanee Ramlochan

Mervyn Taylor tells the story of the
owl in the Rockefeller Christmas tree,
the giant tree arriving prostrate, dragged
by its feet, gift-wrapped in pea green paper.
They found her, eyes startled, feathers bark,
hungry, and the worker wondered if he
was imagining, like that time as a
child when some kids swore they saw it, screamed
in the schoolyard. Imagination. Maybe
this is how fate corrects the chaos of
a tree's felling, with an owl. And maybe this
owl is like your poems: hunting by night,
a parliament of talons, heads spiraling,
each a candle that buds before dying.
Bring light, bring wind, rip words from
others, because in our city of rain-washed
histories, all the trees are falling. Dearest,
you promised me poems.

A Movie Whose Title We've Long Forgotten

shows on the television set that has been moved aside to
the corner of the room where we children huddle around
it while parents lime in the drawing room sipping ponche
a crème and rum. The same movie was on the previous
year when we visited Aunty B in Paramin and the steep
ascent of the road was like parang music, jolting us above
the mist as players pranced from house to house decked
in green, gold, and red. It was the claymation one, the
movie, the one with Rudolph and the Abominable Snow
Monster and the Island of Misfit Toys, you remember it,
right? It was on TTT the year we stayed up late to go to
midnight mass, the house smelling of ham and
sweetbread while someone outside burst bamboo, the
one in which something was forever happening, some
story involving antlers budding from bright hair and
Santa's misfit elves running away, and just as their
pudding bodies were fixed yet molten clay, so too our
lamb-like selves are glued to the screen, each frame
savoured the way a pastelle filled with meat and olives is
sliced and eaten, the way a poem is read line by line, as
adults perfume themselves in other rooms while
poinsettias bleed glorious red wine and we become drunk
on the sense of repetition, the sense of an unending
procession of scenes following what came before, what
comes next: reindeer flying, stars like tinsel, a bright red
nose, a Latin mass, incense rising, an altar with pieces
that move as the wicked monster falls into a white chasm
of ice. And Rudolph is not flawed, not weak, his bright red
difference is his immaculate strength and soft horns have
become a crown that will be worn, like a beloved silver
brooch, each year, each time, again and again so that we
may remember that Christmas Eve and the laughter on
the hill.

The Gifts

I remember the Christmas we went to the beach,
    the waves sweeping up rumours with broken glass.
I remember the Christmas we painted the accent wall, its pattern
    jagged, asymmetrical, a garden of forked paths.
I remember the Christmas I heard *parang* for the first time, a
    Spanish voice on the radio crying across the gulf.
I remember the Christmas we found a white tree in Excellent City
    and I wondered privately whether it was politically
    correct to have a white tree in a country without snow.
I remember the Christmas the poinsettia died.
I remember the Christmas we rang out the false and rang in
    the true.
I remember the Christmas I sat on the cold floor of the room
    I shared with my sister and held my new truck. It was red,
    white and blue, and I could tell Daddy was not happy,
    I could tell he did not love you. And still
I remember the Christmas when everything he touched turned to
    cigarette ash.
I remember the Christmas we dismantled the tree, putting its
    poems back into boxes, because the next day we had to
    move.
I remember the Christmas I looked at the candle and someone
    came and kissed me, no footsteps, no voice, lips unseen.
I remember the Christmas that was not really Christmas, but
    Carnival. People were liming in houses, going to fetes,
    dancing to soca, and each body was its own ornament.
I remember the Christmas I baked cookies and watched
    It's a Wonderful Life and there were hints of murder
    in James Stewart's eyes.
I remember the Christmas I looked at our tree, on which every
    finger had its ring, and felt there was no tomorrow
    but then the doors in the house opened into other
    scenes—some recounted, some foretold—and the
    gifts were waiting.

The White Christmas Tree

It came from the Pearl River Delta of China
where, in a plant of 50 workers, the culture of plastic finds perfection:
flat strips of polyvinyl chloride, unraveled film reels,
are bonded together before a circular blade slices them,
shredding them into needles that are twisted
around metal and then pulled through an excruciating coil.
And then the branches are
                                        cut to size by hand,
bouquets sewn together with polypropylene twine,
and sharp edges bent to stop children from hurting themselves.
All that is left is to attach the branches to the metal trunks.
And to place each segment of our dissected white tree,
the Damien Hirst shark parts, into a coffin-like box
that is put into a truck and driven to a shipping container
bigger than each worker's house.
A crane places the container on board, where it slumbers amid
unsolved rubix cubes, and the vessel sails over the sea.
It could go anywhere really: past India and Sri Lanka,
around the horn of Africa, through the Suez Canal,
or past the Cape of Good Hope and over The Middle Passage,
or across the Pacific, past the dragons on Galapagos,
and through the Panama Canal.
But it arrives in the Caribbean Sea
where warm water warms itself,
water lapping the boat, water rising to light like a dolphin rising to the sky,
then falling again like thoughts.
At the port of Port of Spain, they open the present, the tree
is taken to a warehouse, where it swells in the heat for months.
At length, it is wanted, roused, and taken
through a city of zinc roofs and frangipani trees,
into a town named after a silk cotton tree: Mucurapo.
It is here we find what the store attendants have
assembled, seemingly just for us, at the top of the stairs.

We return with it to our apartment,
the place we've moved into only eight months ago.
No fragrant pine needles that shed, no green-dyed goose feathers,
this plastic dream is now here in our living room with its
adjacent colonised territories:
one worshipful chair, one embarrassed lamp,
a few bashful curtains through which neighbours might peep,
and us
standing before it, our separate natures blending into a sphere
the white and the white of Plato's shell.
O Christmas tree, great unrooted blossomer,
Are you the leaf, the blossom or the bole?
Are you the baubles, the lights, the silver stag horns?
Are you the water which, once crossed,
you no longer drink?
Are you the joy we will never shed?

Poem on My 40th Birthday

I will never have children. I will never own a house.
I will never solve my family's problems.
I will never see the Pacific Ocean
or Paris or Rome or Australia.
I will never be an American.
I will never be British. Or Jamaican. It is too late
to learn the Russian language. I will
never have Instagram-ready pecs. I cannot grow orchids.
I will never be married.
I will never become an astronaut. I will never be prime minister.
Or president. Or an MP.
I cannot know if my dog really loves me.
No one will ever hear me sing.
I will never direct a film or compose a symphony.
There is no time to author the novel.
I will never attend the opera.
I will not become a dancer.
I will never have a solo exhibition or a grand opening where my friends gather and sip
wine and talk about their enemies.
No one will read my poems. No one will read my stories.
No one will know of my essays or opinions.
Yoga classes in the Savannah will elude me.
I will never be cool.
None of my friends will ever spontaneously drive me to the beach.
Hiking lush hills for pleasure will escape me. As will quiet walks
among the daffodils. I will never touch a hummingbird.
You will never read my nature poem.
I will never earn enough to do a PhD.
I will never be prepared for
death. This poem, I will never hold.

On Translating Florentino y el Diablo

In the classic Venezuelan poem *Florentino and the Devil*
the word *coplero* appears in the first line and I wonder if the word
means what it looks like: couple, couplet, cup—as though Florentino and the
Devil are lovers: Florentino a twink, the Devil his *papi chulo*
and the concatenation of the poem a kind of intercourse, the
joropo a dance of feet. In my translation, they meet on Grindr, naturally,
each a *caminante sin camino*, walker without path, singing all
night to harp and maracas, the careful give and take of terms, conditions.

Yet, somehow it is not the men who are the real subjects of Torrealba's
poem. Other words jump at me: *cielo, rio, terraplén, sabana*—words
thrown from a lonesome geography, a llanos of pain in which Mora trees
drop their seeds like tears, and rivers carry them to Trinidad, my island,
where forests fill with saplings and the full valleys declare, in new Latin,
the mating complete, the border drowned, the challenge finally satisfied.

Misreading Florentino y el Diablo

Sin vacadani corcel	A horse! a horse! my kingdom for my horse!
Una con mi alma en la sola	The soul is the prison of the body.
la voz por la sala cruza	A lie can travel half way around the world while the truth is putting on its shoes.
canto major cuando vuelo	a pond versed in streaming
aspiran los que la ven	a tree dreaming of blooming
Ecos lejanos repiten	Come to me in the silence of the night
como el odiar y el querer	eternity

On Hermann Hesse's Narcissus and Goldmund, *1930*

circles and we don't even know that we are going around in

Writing through Siddhartha

how? how you said
  — John Cage, *Writing through Finnegans Wake*
the words came flowing to him
  — Hermann Hesse, *Siddhartha*

a bird or
a bird's appetite
a bit
a bit denser every day
a bit different
a bit heavier
a bit murkier every month
a bit silly yes
a bit strange
a bizarre
a blessing
a blossom
a boat
a bottomless pit

thus without reason
time
Time is
time she
times
times but
Timid
timidly fled
timidness
tiny
tired
tired mouth
tiredness
tiredness came over Siddhartha
tiredness has overwhelmed me

his ardent will
his arms
his arms folded
his arms were hanging down
his beard
his breath
his business-deals
his chest
his companion
his counterpart
his course
his dormant spirit suddenly woke up
his entire body like the lukewarm
his entire long sleep had been nothing but
his eyes
his eyes became motionless
his eyes fixed
his eyes were fixed on
his eyes were rigidly focused towards
his eyes were starting
his face
his farewell
his fate
his father
his father appeared
his father felt
his father had said
his father's son
his fear
his fears flowed
his feet
his finger closed her eyelids
his forehead
his friend
his futile fight against them
his future is already
his gestures
His glance turned
his goal

His goal attracts him
his greeting
his guest while asking
his heart
his heart felt cold
his heart full
his heart his own life
his high calling
his landlords business
his liberated
his life had been
His life had indeed been strange
his mind
his mind becoming one with
his mockery had become more tired
his mother sang
his mouth twitched
his own image
his own knowledge
his own search
his own search able
his own suffering
his pain will be
his path
his path had passed through life
his power
his quietly dangling hand
his quietly lowered glance
his respect
his self
his self had flown into the oneness
his self had retreated
His senses
his senses had become alive
his servant
his shadow
his shoulders
his skin
his small

his smile
his smile became more similar
his smile shone golden
his solid staff
his son
his son appeared
his soul
his soul die
his soul sent after the Brahman as
his spear-carrier
his spell
his suffering was
his superiority had become more
his teachings
his teachings be strange
his teachings sound foolish
his thighs
his walk
his way against her
his will was
His wound blossomed
his yellow cloak

Siddhartha's ear
Siddhartha's eyes
Siddhartha's eyes read the suffering
Siddhartha's face
Siddhartha's hand
Siddhartha's interest
Siddhartha's previous births were
Siddhartha's shoulder
Siddhartha's soul slipped inside the body

everything always becomes
everything came back
everything can be learned
everything could be
everything else
everything enter his mind
everything has
everything has existence
everything is
everything is Brahman
everything is coming
everything is easy
everything is one-sided which can be thought
everything is perfect
everything only
everything shown
everything was

Super Blue Blood Moon Valentine

it was full moon but not an ordinary full moon and somehow the night was blacker than usual and that just made the moon's light so much more magnetic and the sea was churning and really it was like watching silver leaf being crumpled and he had this act where he pulled out a glass ball and I was astounded because of the rum punch yet there was some degree of uncertainty as to how I was going to get home but the Midnight Robber told me there was a gay fete going on across the street and I think he wanted me to come with him and I wanted him but I didn't know if tonight I could feel safe I never feel safe I wanted to swim and feel safe like the time I went skinny dipping with my cousins and I think that was how they told me they loved me

Acknowledgements

Poems first appeared in: *Anthropocene, Beltway Poetry Quarterly, Fourteen Poems, harana poetry, Hawai'i Review, Magma Poetry, PN Review, The Abandoned Playground, Wild Court,* and *WritersMosaic*. 'Mirrors' was published in *I Wanna Be Loved by You: Poems on Marilyn Monroe*, edited by Susana H. Case and Margo Taft Stever (Milk & Cake Press, 2022). 'Writing through *Siddhartha*' is extracted from a longer sequence inspired by John Cage's experiments with famous texts and involving the use of the JanusNode computer program, first published in pamphlet form by Broken Sleep in 2021. 'A Movie Whose Title We've Long Forgotten' first appeared in *Christmas Movies*, edited by Di Slaney and Katherine Towers (Candlestick Press, 2021), while 'The Gifts' appeared in *Christmas Presents*, also published by Candlestick in 2020. 'Carnival Bat' first appeared in *Battalion*, edited by Kirsten Irving and Jon Stone (Sidekick Books, 2018).

'Chapter One' is an erasure of the opening pages of Samuel Selvon's novel *Turn Again Tiger* (Heinemann, 1979 [1958]). Readers may recognise that 'Tropopause – a Cento' is derived from Shakespeare's *King Lear* and that 'Secondary Circulation – a Cento' is generated from Robert Frost's poems 'Storm Fear' and 'A Line-storm Song'. 'Cento from a Poet from the British Virgin Islands' is taken from the work of Richard Georges, specifically his book *Epiphaneia* (Out-Spoken Press, 2019). The opening poem's title is with apologies to Eve Kosofsky Sedgwick.

Thank you, Aaron Kent, Charlie Baylis, Robert Selby, Ben Townley-Canning, Philip Terry, Michael Schmidt, Leo Boix, Nathalie Teitler, LynleyShimat Lys, Marley Aiu, Daniele Pantano, Indran Amirthanayagam, Sara Cahill Marron, Monique Roffey, Gabriel Gbadamosi, Kostya Tsolakis, Di Slaney, Katherine Towers, Kirsten Irving, Jon Stone Nicholas Laughlin, Andil Gosine, Susana H. Case, Mervyn Taylor, Rajiv Mohabir, Zain Aslam, Jee Leong Koh, Karen McCarthy Woolf, Mona Arshi, J. Vijay Maharaj, Alison Donnel, Nathan Hamilton, and Chaplin, for assisting with poetry readings over the years.

LAY OUT YOUR UNREST

www.ingramcontent.com/pod-product-compliance
Lightning Source LLC
Chambersburg PA
CBHW021938040426
42448CB00008B/1135